Yiddish
for
Yankees

Martin Marcus

Yiddish for

J. B. Lippincott Company

Philadelphia / New York

Yankees

or, Funny, You Don't Look Gentile

To Susie

Contents

Yiddish for Yankees

THIS BOOK IS FOR GENTILES AND JEWS BOTH. It is Must reading for Jews because it gives away all kinds of secrets. And what Jew doesn't want to know which secrets are being told to whom, because Jews have no secrets in the first place, and even if they did, who would be interested?

The truth is, the Jews do have one enormous secret: how they have managed to laugh all these miserable thousands of years, and why shouldn't all of America finally be let in on the longest private joke in history? That private joke is the subject of this book. The Jewish sense of humor, inspired by Yiddish, is really one of the Jews' greatest gifts to American culture. It is about time the gift was unwrapped.

To the Gentiles in the audience! Let's face it, these are the Sinking Sixties and we are all in the same lifeboat. Yiddish humor is lifeboat humor, for centuries—of necessity—a desperate sort of humor, a way to put down the whole *cockamehmeh* world. This book tells you what a *cockamehmeh* world is. And how to put it down. At long last, Yiddish humor is "in," not just for Jews but for everybody. No matter whether you're a blueblood or a Red Guard or a Goldwater, you need a Yiddish point of view as a sort of emotional fallout shelter, a second wind for the Rat Race. It's the Universal Defense Mechanism. And now that other non-Jews are already busily defending themselves with Jewish jibes and Yiddish yaks, why should you be verbally unarmed in the face of H-bombs, Chinese hordes and such? While others laugh their melancholy Jewish laughs, why should you be left standing there with nothing but a Gentile look on your face?

The first step to a Yiddish point of view is, of course, a Yiddish vocabulary. Not the kind you get from dictionaries or books by giggly Jewish matrons, but an up-to-date, pronounceable vocabulary that describes bridge partners who trump your aces. That puts new life into tired office repartee. That lifts the world from your Ivy League shoulders, the kids out of your hair, and the spouse off your back.

And here it is! In these pages, the greatest inside lingo of all time, Yiddish, in easy-to-learn form especially for swinging Gentiles. Startle your friends. Annoy your enemies. Be the hit of commuter rides, church socials and Junior League meetings. Feel comfortable in Jewish delicatessens. Here are words to describe great calamities. Words to differentiate between ordinary misery and catastrophe. Colorful curses! Acid apothegms! Incomprehensible innuendo! In short, a fresh, new vocabulary for cynics of every race, creed or color.

This small lexicon will vex some Yiddish-speaking readers. They will beat their foreheads with chagrin. They will say the spelling is wrong, the pronunciations are wrong, the definitions are wrong. (As of this moment my own mother is not speaking to me.) They will call me names, but they will use the very names you find in these chapters, regardless of the spelling. The reader may be assured, however, that each of the expressions herein has been approved by at least two "authorities," which is about as much agreement as you can find among Jewish people on any subject.*

Note: The words as they appear in parentheses are spelled phonetically. Italics indicate accented syllables. There is no English equivalent for the "ch" sound. It's a little like clearing your throat, pronounced the same as in the Scottish word "loch." In pronunciations, "g" is hard, as in "gander."

* See Certified Mavins' Page.

Certified
Mavins' Page

*(In acknowledgment to the wise old bearded scholars
who helped make this book possible . . .*
Jerry Barnbaum
Morrie Korengold
Gert Korengold
Raymond B. Young
*. . . and several minor chochems their feelings shouldn't
be hurt but they didn't help that much).*

You should live like
an onion with
your head in the ground.

1.

A

Thousand

Finks

Yiddish has a name for every fool, jackass or rotten swine you ever met. Some you never met. This chapter must necessarily be one of the longest of the book. Even so, it fails miserably to catalogue the vast army of imbeciles and poops who populate our everyday world.

shlemiel (shluh *meal*)   A jerk. A person with crazy plans, like wanting you to invest your life savings in a scheme he has to grow pineapples in Oregon.

shmegehgeh (shmuh *geh* gee)   A SHLEMIEL who tried last year to grow pineapples in Oregon, this year he's trying bananas.

shlemazel (shluh *mah* zul)   An unlucky SHLEMIEL who couldn't grow pineapples in Hawaii, let alone Oregon.

goylem (*goy* lum)   A big dummy. A person who would go into business with a SHLEMIEL. ·

shtoonk (shtoonk)   A nogood; a stinker. Someone who does you dirty. Could be your own brother even.

momser (*mom* zer)   An s.o.b. A plain old dirty rotten skunk who would cut your heart out for a nickel.

yoksh (yawksh)   A buffoon. There is the true story of the groom who appeared at the bridal shower and was so thrilled with one of the gifts—an electric picture—that for twenty minutes he ran around searching for an outlet, sweating and crooning, "Isn't it terrific!" The groom was a YOKSH.

nebach (*neh* bach)   A colorless person; a nobody. Has been described as a poor soul who enters a room and creates the impression that someone has just left.

goniff (*gah* niff)   A crook by birth. The neighbor who steals your parking place. The woman who is wearing the same dress as you, and other pathological criminals.

11

klutz (klutts)   A clumsy oaf. A guest who sits on your antique coffee table and breaks the legs, she should break her own legs once.

zhlob (zhlawb)   A big fat rude slob. The animal neighbor who drops in for a chat and eats your dinner for his dessert.

chochem (*chaw* chem)   Literally, a wise man. Use it to describe that person who has everything figured out, knows all the answers before anyone else, and has never once in his life been right about anything at all.

kunnilemmel (koo nee *lem* mul)   A person of low mentality. You wouldn't let him run the store for a minute, he might sell the cash register.

shtick fetts (*shtick* fets)   A big piece of fat. Useful in describing a person you don't care for who happens to be obese.

parech (parch)   The sufferer of a skin disease or the disease itself (alopecia). Useful in describing a person you don't care for who happens to be bald.

macher (*mah* cher)   A big shot; a wheeler-dealer. Your brother, an unemployed forty-two-year-old-PARECH who is going to make a killing this year in second-hand hearing aids. Last year, with your money, he made a killing in reject budgiebirds.

Moishe Kapour (*moy* sheh keh *pore*)   A poor slob who does everything backwards. I believe it was Sam Levinson who described him as a fellow who spends a night at a hotel and leaves his own towel.

yenteh (*yen* teh)   A gossip; a busybody. A third cousin who asks you at a bar mitzvah so what's your salary and why aren't you giving money for Uncle Morris in the old peoples' home in Milwaukee?

yachneh (*yahch* neh)   A YENTEH who *knows* your salary and why you're not supporting Uncle Morris, and talks about nothing else, and never stops talking.

nudnik (*nude* nick)   A goof; a nuisance. Someone who is always pinching and touching you. He not only talks with his hands, he talks with your clothes and even your skin.

mishugeneh (mih *shuh* geh neh)   A crazy person; a crackpot. A teen-age daughter who would go out on the street in winter without even a sweater under her coat.

fizehnish (fih *zay* nish)   A monster; an ugly individual. Your daughter in Hollywood, California, sends you a snapshot of her fiancé. He's not a movie star so he's a FIZEHNISH.

alteh kocker (*ahl* teh *cock* ker)   A.K. for short. An old poop; a fuddyduddy. Not only isn't your daughter's fiancé a movie star, he's at least thirty-two years old, an A.K. already.

shnorer (*shnaw* rer)   A freeloader; a mooch. An unmarried cousin from Detroit who brings you flower seeds in November, he'll wait until April so he should see your face when they bloom.

mavin (*may* vin)   A specialist; an expert. This cousin he's a MAVIN also. He lives in the same city with General Motors so naturally he's a car MAVIN.

farmekeh (*far* meh key)   A farm woman; an ungainly, unstylish female. "So what kind of dates is your son going to have in a place like Cambridge, Massachusetts? FARMEKEHS?"

fehgeleh (*fay* guh luh)   A little bird. Popularly, a very sweet young man. Very sweet. You know, a FEHGELEH!

krechs (krechs)   A groaner; a malcontent. If there's a silver lining he'll find the black cloud.

shtimmer (*shtim* mer)   A deaf mute. Your own child when you holler on him where has he been until all hours of the night and he gives you only a look. "Speak, SHTIMMER," you say.

grobber (*graw* ber)   An uncouth person. The same child, he reaches across the dinner table for a handful of American fried potatoes, you smack his hand. "Hands off, GROBBER," you say.

hoyber (*hoy* ber)   A hunchback; a poor physical specimen; a pitiful sight. What, from so much bending down and picking up, every Jewish mother complains she is becoming.

dorfying (*dorf* yink)   A country bumpkin; a rube. Any resident of Florida who isn't from Miami Beach.

ahkshin (*ahk* shin)   A stubborn jackass. Your own husband, he'll install bicycle pedals before he'll buy a new car.

verbrennter (fur *bren* ter)   A fiery-eyed radical; an extremist. Your cousin, the SHTIMMER, has a couple drinks wine and he's standing on the table giving a speech in favor of free love. Suddenly he's a VERBRENNTER.

14

balaguleh   (bah la *goo* leh)   A truck driver. A man whose only qualification for work is a strong back. The guy in the next office who was just promoted.

shlump   (shlump)   A slow, slovenly person; a sad sack. What you feel like the day you wear your shiny suit and ratty tie to the office and the chairman of the board pops in for an all-day conference.

ferimmter   (fur *rim* ter)   An egomaniac; a showoff. An old high school pal you haven't seen for twenty years who shows up with all his hair and a waistline like Mr. Universe.

gazlan   (*gahs* lun)   Your own personal tormenter. An individual who was brought into the world for the sole purpose of aggravating you to death.

klippa   (*klip* puh)   A troublemaking wife; a relentless nag. You could be on an expedition in search of rare amphibious animals deep in the Okefenokee wilderness, and a helicopter would fly overhead and drop you a telephone, it's your KLIPPA, you didn't fix the bedroom screen.

vildechi   (*vill* deh chee)   A wild woman. The distant cousin who shows up at the wedding uninvited and describes, for everybody's ears, long-forgotten and imaginary family grievances.

pisher   (*pih* sher)   One who wets his pants; hence, anybody who is too young for his responsibilities. A doctor under thirty-five years of age is a PISHER. Elderly men who marry young women are ALTEH KOCKERS who marry PISHERS.

lemishkeh (*leh* mish keh) A wishy-washy person; a drag. LEMISHKEHS are people you invite to a party and who have to know "Who's going to be there?" "Is there someplace to park my car?" "Will there be a lot of drinking?" . . . You wonder why you invited them in the first place.

beyzon (*bay* zuhn) Beasts of burden. "The Chicago Bears today drafted two defensive halfbacks, three quarterbacks and five BEYZON."

bummerkeh (*bum* mer keh) A lady bum. What your thirteen-year-old daughter looks like in her fishnet stockings and tiger-striped underwear.

Poilisheh (*poy* lih sheh) A Polish person. Yiddish is totally nondiscriminatory in its terms for races and nationalities. Irishmen are IRISHERS; Italians are TALLENERS (tah *len* ners); Negroes are SHVARTZES (*shvahr* tzehs); and Jews are YIDDEN—all equally derogatory.

shmuck (shmuck) What can I tell you? This is one of the few dirty names in Yiddish. And a SHMEKELEH (*shmeh* keh leh) is a littler one.

putz (putts) Another such name for the same kind of person. Or, a PETZIE, if you prefer diminutives.

cham (chahm) The most foolish of all the fools. Sometimes in describing a fool it is necessary to include his family, his teacher and his ancestors. CHAM does that very nicely.

16

vergrebter (fur *grep* ter) An ignoramus. What some people will call the author of this book.

goyisheh kopf (*goy* ish eh *kawp*) Literally, a Gentile head. A person who is easily duped, who does not catch on. What you will not be after reading this book.

The bride is older than my grandmother.

2.

And A Few Good People (Maybe)

It is more difficult in Yiddish to compliment someone than to insult him. Even the kindest words have cynical undertones. For example, if you call your brother-in-law a terrific provider, you imply at the same time that things are not so hot at home.

You may say that a woman is beautiful and, without adding another word, leave the impression that beautiful is all she is. The few examples in this chapter will give you the idea.

balabusta (bah la *bus* teh) Quite a woman; a champion homemaker and mother. If applied, however, to a young modern housewife this could mean a girl who thinks the only thing you do with a bed is make it.

gezinteh (geh *zin* teh) A healthy person. If your own husband has an ulcer, cholesterol, a hernia and flat feet, he's a sickly man. Your sister's husband, he's only got gallstones and prostate, she married a GEZINTEH.

bullvant (bull *vahnt*) A man with the build of an ox; a strongman. Any neighbor your wife says you should punch in the nose for playing the hi-fi too loud who's over five foot six.

lantzman (*lahnts* man) A fellow countryman. Someone who grew up in the same city or neighborhood as you. A good person to do business with if you're looking for it. A good person to avoid if you're not.

nahfkeh (*noff* key) A married man's ladyfriend. Nothing so serious as a mistress. She is more nearly a trifle, a plaything. You wouldn't want your wife to know about her, but on the other hand, she's of such small importance it doesn't hurt your conscience.

shamus (*shah* mus)   The caretaker of the synagogue. Yiddish has a contempt for titles, and the word has come to include almost anybody who is "in charge." Cops, guards, bus drivers, first sergeants, mother-in-laws . . . SHAMUS describes them all.

grosser philisoph (*gro* ser fih luh *sahf*)   An important philosopher. Any person with fancy ideas, like a "sure-fire" plan to end the traffic problem, he can't understand why the authorities haven't thought of it.

gottseliger (got *seh* lih gur)   A holy person. If you, yourself, are not such a religious individual, it could mean anyone who goes to church more than once a month. Or someone who goes less than once a month, but writes a big check more than once a year.

edel mensch (*ay* dul mensh)   A gentleman. Or, a young man of such refined manners you wouldn't want him to date your daughter, because if he got sexy, how could you tell her to kick such a person in the groin?

typewriterkeh (typewriter keh)   Harry Golden illustrates how Yiddish can take an innocent English word and make it sarcastic. For instance, if your daughter takes a typist's job instead of finishing college, you sigh and say she's a TYPEWRITERKEH, or a STENOGRAPHERRN. Yiddish diminutives tend to put little needles on the ends of English words. And you can make up your own: My son, the EXECUTIVENIK; his brother, the MECHANICKER.

haymisheh (*hay* mih sheh)   A word to describe a comfortable, homey kind of person. To a mother, a HAYMISHEH fella is a solid family man. To a daughter, he's a square.

shaifeleh (*shay* feh leh) A dear, innocent little child; a lamb. Your son in high school. The one the authorities are trying to tell you is responsible for hiding a closed circuit TV camera in the girls' shower room.

It should smell
from your head.

3.

From Bad
to Worse
to
Vershtoonkeneh

How are things with you anyway? Pretty
rotten? Life getting too complicated for
you? Maybe you drink too much, or your
husband's feet smell, or you're cutting paper
dolls out of stock certificates. The Yiddish
words in this chapter will help you to laugh

your way through life's everyday irritations and disappointments. They're funnier than the familiar four-letter words, and frequently more discerning.

verblonget (fur *blawn* jet) Lost; hopelessly confused. You lost all your money at the track, your wife told you she's expecting, you found somebody else's name on your office, and you learn your psychiatrist just shot himself. Can you think of a better word than VERBLONGET?

vermisht (fur *misht*) Mixed up in the head. You drive off the turnpike into a gas station because all your five kids have to go to the john at once, and you find there's a line. You are VERMISHT.

tsedrehteh (tseh *dray* teh) Double VERMISHT; crazy in the head. Same gas station, same kids, only one of them can't wait and you discover you have to go yourself.

tzimmis (*tsim* iss) Literally a vegetable stew. An aggravating, mucked-up situation. You're in your GAHTKEHS,* watching a crucial ballgame on TV, when unexpectedly your wife's whole family from St. Louis pops in. A surprise? No, a TZIMMIS!

mishegas (mish shuh *gahs*) A craziness. Something really foolish or complicated. While your wife's family from St. Louis are making themselves at home, the furnace explodes, the baby swallows a clothespin, you get a call from your NAHFKEH, the dog eats the chopped liver and *your* family from Pittsburgh drops in. This is a MISHEGAS.

* You don't know what GAHTKEHS are already, so you'll peek on page 33.

shikker (*shik* ker) Drunk or a drunken person. A teetotaler's word, always used disapprovingly. You are SHIKKER whether you have a second glass of Mogen David wine on Passover or a fifth of hard booze every night and pass out.

verfnyifkit (fur *fnyiff* kit) Plastered. Just another funny one to add to your collection of falling-down-drunk words.

cockamehmeh (*kah* kuh may mee) Junky; poorly or foolishly conceived. You and your COCKAMEHMEH ideas. She and her COCKAMEHMEH friends. The neighbors and their COCKAMEHMEH barbecues.

shlock (shlock) Sleazy; cheap or badly run. A fly-by-night business is a SHLOCK operation. If you fly tourist, you say first class is extravagant. If all you can get is first class, you dismiss all lesser accommodations as SHLOCK.

zoftik (*zoff* tick) Soft and springy. A very nice word when applied to young ladies, meaning a surplus of epidermis in the right places. An insult when applied to your brain.

meescheit (*mee* iss chite) You're single? This is a word to describe the blind date who is not merely homely or ugly in the ordinary sense. Her face is a tragedy. She is ugliness personified. She is MEESCHEIT!

gehshtruft (geh *shtruhft*) Accursed; born unlucky. There's the story of the two businessmen, Max and Harry. Max prayed every Friday night in the temple and his business flouished. Harry, the GEHSHTRUFTER, prayed every Monday, Wednesday, and Friday, but his business failed. "Lord," he said, "this is how you treat a man who prays three times a week?" A heavenly voice responded, "You bug me, Harry."

kinehora (kin neh *haw* ruh) A curse in reverse. A colleague says with best intentions, "Looks like you're going to get a promotion, Jack." KINEHORA! You quick cover his mouth, to utter such a thing is to assure it will never happen.

ahftseloches (ahf tseh *law* chus) Inevitable bad luck. The result of a KINEHORA. The boss calls you in to tell you of your promotion and your fly is wide open. AHFTSELOCHES, you think. Something like this had to happen!

chalerya (cha *lair* yuh) Literally, cholera. A plague of curses. You're on the plane to Florida. You couldn't get a room at the Fontainebleau, you had to pay $50 for your wife's excess baggage, the kids are airsick, and the pilot announces it's snowing in Miami. A CHALERYA!

finsternish (*fin* stir nish) A darkness; a gloom; a depressing or ominous feeling in the air. "Every time Mary Anne enters the room, a FINSTERNISH comes in with her."

ungehpotchkeyed (*ung* geh potch keed*) Messed up; fussy; overdone. Your daughter wears lipstick, powder and eyeshadow, she looks like a lady. Her daughter wears lipstick, powder, eyeshadow *and* false eyelashes, she looks UNGEHPOTCHKEYED.

nisht gefehrlach (nisht geh *fair* lach) Not so terrible. Your big deal fell through, they gave you a closet for your new office, and you think you have an ulcer. So your wife says, "NISHT GEFEHRLACH, you should hear what kind of a day *I* had."

bloteh (*blaw* teh) A swamp. A cesspool. In your wife's eyes what the house has become while you took care of the kids all afternoon.

* Exception. Pronounce the "ch" as in "hitched."

oysgamitched (*oys* guh mitched*) Absolutely pooped out. So tired as to be hanging between life and death. After a long night of drinking and partying, you wobble into the office the next morning. You tell your secretary, "If anybody phones, tell them I'm OYSGAMITCHED."

beregitz (buh *ray* gits) Peeved and frustrated. On the way to the theater you are stopped and ticketed for a minor traffic violation. The officer chooses this time to deliver a one-hour lecture on driver responsibility. As you squirm in your bucket seat, the curtain falls on Act One. You are BEREGITZ.

blechedich (*bleh* cheh dich) Lifeless; sickly. You are just getting over a bad case of stomach flu when the ship you are on hits rough seas and you discover they are serving boiled rabbit for lunch. You feel BLECHEDICH.

vershtoonkeneh (fur *shtoonk* ken neh) Stinking. You and your VERSHTOONKENEH ideas. She and her VERSHTOONKENEH friends. The neighbors and their VERSHTOONKENEH barbecues.

vershtickt (fur *shtikt*) Choking, gagging. The feeling you get when diapering someone else's baby, or evaluating a competitor's product.

verkockteh (fur *kock* teh) A ribald word meaning worse than crappy. No offense, but this book wouldn't be complete if I didn't include it.

farfallen (far *fah* len) Describes a lost cause; a hopeless case. Your child (the one destined to be a brilliant surgeon) flunks kindergarten. It's FARFALLEN.

* Exception. Pronounce the "ch" as in "hitched."

nedugehdach   (neh *doo* geh dahch)   Without a doubt the most forlorn word in any language. A profound pity. An unthinkable catastrophe. My mother's definition is as good as any. A NEDUGEHDACH, she says, is something so terrible "it shouldn't happen in this county!"

Instant

Martyrdom

Take any everyday English verb. The word "buy," for example. In English, you buy something, you buy something. But in Yiddish the word is charged with dramatic implications. You didn't just buy something. You spent your last dollar that your child

You should live like a chandelier... hang by day, burn by night.

should have a warm new winter outfit. Or consider the simple act of walking. "Do you walk to the shopping center?" someone asks. "I walk," you answer. With my rheumatism, flat feet, varicose veins, three blocks I walk up and back every day, my husband wouldn't buy a second car. In Yiddish you can bend over to tie your shoelace, and when you straighten up, you are a martyr!

shlep   (shlep)   To drag. Not merely to move an object, but to accept a greater burden than any person should be expected to. One who SHLEPS, whether it is his family from Europe or the laundry up from the basement, is a martyr in the truest sense.

kvetch   (kvech*)   To complain. To gripe with noxious persistence. KVETCHING is the right of every woman, no matter how well off she is, to let other women know that life isn't too easy for her.

nudge   (nooj)   To bother. To make a nuisance of yourself. Your husband is enjoying himself with a good book. You NUDGE him about vacation plans for 1974, he shouldn't be too content.

plotz   (plots)   To explode. To fall apart as with laughter or overeating. At your mother's dinner you have two choices: to eat like a normal human being and disgrace her, or to eat as she tells you and PLOTZ.

* Exception. Pronounce the "ch" as in "China."

pager (*pay* gur)   To die a martyred death. The weather is so hot you could PAGER. Or the weather is so cold you could PAGER. Or your son in medical school drops out and enlists for six years in the merchant marine. You PAGER.

tseshmetter (tseh *shmeh* ter)   To smash into pieces. To clobber. "What happened to the Mets today?" "They were TSESHMETTERED!"

zager (*zay* gur)   To connive. To play the angles. The guy in the next office who started the same day you did gets three weeks' vacation. You only get one. Let's face it, fella, he knows how to ZAGER.

shpritz (shprits)   To spray. Just a nice little word to describe when you're talking to someone named Schuster or Schlesinschloss, and you make wet on him.

kibbitz (*kih* bits)   To offer unwanted advice. Frequently a cause of justified homicide. For instance, it's ten below zero on a lonely road and you're looking under the hood of your stalled automobile, when your wife says, "I told you last September we needed a new car."

shmei (shmy)   To gossip, but with relish. You may keep your secretary late every night, and people will gossip. But when the boss is discovered with the receptionist in the utility closet, ah, that's something to SHMEI about.

shtop (shtawp)   To stuff until bursting. A rich neighbor woman SHTOPS her house with furniture. And—if that same woman is promiscuous—you might say she SHTOPS!

fumfer (*foom* fur)· To stutter; to act hesitantly as though reluctant to get to the point. No matter what your politics, you must admit that President Johnson FUMFERS.

grepps (greps) To belch. But, as with most every common verb in Yiddish, to do so with deep, dramatic meaning. To belch with style.

bupkeh (*boop* keh) To chatter and cluck like a chicken. If a woman spends forty minutes in the powder room, she's BUPKEHING. If a man does, he's in trouble.

yentz (yents) To sharp somebody, especially in business. To YENTZ is not necessarily dishonest. I am reminded of a saying familiar to retail merchants in central Pennsylvania: "We will not cheat thee, but we will do our best to outwit thee." That's Quaker talk for "What's the fun of being in business if you can't YENTZ a little?"

Take care
Where the horse was standing
it is very slippery.

5.

The Queen's Underwear and Other Impertinences

Even the words to describe the small odds and ends of life were coined with sarcasm by the people who found it necessary to invent Yiddish. Hence, it's hard to say "stomach" without saying "big fat stomach." And whatever humor there is in a hernia is captured by the Yiddish word for it. Yiddish is an earthy, impertinent tongue. It makes no class distinctions. It doesn't fool around with euphemisms. No other language is so designed to humble the haughty and remove the stuffing from the stuffed-shirt.

gahtkehs (*got* keys)　Long underwear. In Yiddish slang, underwear is *long* underwear. It doesn't matter who you are—an old man, a young bride, the Queen of England—what you wear next to your skin is always GAHTKEHS!

shpilkehs (*shpill* keys)　Restlessness. Ants in the pants. You're in the third hour of a four-hour piano recital of children nine to thirteen, and would like to take the potted palm and smash it on your wife's head for dragging you there. You've got SHPILKEHS.

drek (drek)　Junk, crap. All the gifts from the groom's side in the eyes of the bride's mother.

tiniff (*tin* niff)　More junk. All the gifts from the bride's side in the eyes of the groom's mother.

shmateh (*shmah* teh)　A rag. An old, tattered housedress. The one you bought your wife for last New Year's Eve that she never wore again. People in the Garment District refer to their industry as the "SHMATEH business."

sechel (*seh* chel)　Horse sense; "a good head on the shoulders." The daughter who is a Phi Beta Kappa is merely a genius. The one who quit school to marry a doctor has got SECHEL.

tzores (*tsaw* res) Troubles. It's a crazy world. We give the Russians grain, and the Chinese give them TZORES.

boich (boych) The belly. Especially the overhanging kind. Uncle Henry has a BOICH on him. The baby has a BOICH. Even the expectant mother has a BOICH.

kileh (*kill* leh) A hernia. In Yiddish, the universal alibi. Your wife says, "Make me a flagstone patio." "Sure," you say, "and I'll get a KILEH, I'll be in the hospital for three weeks."

pushkeh (*push* key) Any box or receptacle in which money is put. Usually for charity, special savings. Money saved in a PUSHKEH is sacred, never to be touched. Many wealthy families today owe their fortunes to the PUSHKEHS of yesterday.

boobeleh (*boo* beh leh) A precious little jewel. Used as a term of endearment, applied indiscriminately to men, women or children. Willie Mays comes to bat. You shout, "Knock it in the seats, BOOBELEH!"

shandeh (*shahn* deh) A shame; a scandal. God forbid, your wife was unable to get her hair done for the Saturday night bridge party. This is a SHANDEH.

mitzvah (*mits* vah) A blessed event. A birth, a marriage, or even the bridge party being called off when your wife didn't have her hair done.

tsotskeh (*tsots* key) A cheap toy, maybe 29 cents. Something you bring a second cousin's new baby, the big stores weren't open. Or anything cheap and unimportant. Might be a ladyfriend even.

34

Kishnev (*kish* nev) A city in Russia. Any place so far away you don't know or care how to get there. Maybe the suburb your brother-in-law just moved. Or the town in middle Kansas your firm wants to transfer you.

boombeh (*boom* beh) Anything that is too big. A woman wearing a grotesque, oversized diamond brooch wears a BOOMBEH. She may even wear it on her BOOMBEHS.

pulkehs (*pull* keys) Thighs. Usually a woman's large, heavy thighs. When other women wear bikinis they're lovely. When your wife wears a bikini, they're PULKEHS.

chutzpah (*chuts* pah) Colossal nerve. Theo Bikel defines a person with CHUTZPAH as one who murders his parents, then pleads for mercy in court on account he is an orphan.

gehderim (geh *dair* rim) The viscera; your insides. Where it gets you when your brother-in-law complains he owes $5,000 on his new swimming pool.

yenim's pipik (*yeh* nem's *pip* pick) Somebody else's bellybutton. You're just about to sign the check for your income tax when your wife says, "Where will we find the money for the new carpeting?" You suggest she look in YENIM'S PIPIK.

cerebronis (seh reh *braw* nis) Fly specks. Some people get a nice Christmas bonus, some people get CEREBRONIS.

shtick (shtick) Literally a piece. Popularly, a person's specialty or bit. Ladybird Johnson, for instance, is crazy about making the highways nice and pretty. That's her SHTICK. Giving audiences is the Pope's SHTICK. What's your SHTICK?

narishkeit (*nah* rish kite)   Foolishness of the kind that is a nuisance. The car salesman is trying to interest you in power disc brakes, triple carburetors and 900 horsepower engines. "NARISHKEIT!" you tell him. "When I decide to race in the Indianapolis Five Hundred, that's when I'll buy a car from you!"

tochas (*taw* chus)   The buttocks. What a judge sits on all day pounding a hammer, for this he makes such a big salary.

zudik (*zoo* dick)   Another name for the same part of the anatomy. If the judge's decision goes against you, it is customary to wish on him a good case of hemorrhoids or some other malaise of the ZUDIK.

pisha paysha (*pih* sha *pay* sha)   A simple card game. Your bridge partner, in a high-stakes game, misbids a cinch vulnerable grand slam. Rather than cutting his head off at the shoelaces, you wait for your color to return and say, "What game are you playing, sir, PISHA PAYSHA?"

gorgul (*gore* gul)   A funnier word for the throat than throat. "Honey, the kid won't take his medicine." "So shove it down his GORGUL."

shmutz (shmuts)   Dirt. With all the talk from politicians about air and water pollution, maybe if they called it SHMUTZ, they'd do something about it.

shmei drei (*shmy* dry)   Empty talk; baloney. "In his State of the Union address today, the President of the United States told millions of listening Americans a lot of SHMEI DREI."

Donnershtick (*dun* ner shtick) Thursday. In Yiddish, everything can be done on Thursday. Your wife wants to refurnish the whole house. "Sure," you promise her, "next DONNERSHTICK." Or she cries, "When is our daughter ever going to get married?" You answer, "When? On DONNERSHTICK, that's when."

kimpet (*kim* pit) The period of convalescence for a woman after she has given birth. Any person who is laid up for any reason, from hoof and mouth disease to a hangover, you may describe as being "in KIMPET."

pais (*pay* yiss) Long, curling sidelocks worn by certain Orthodox Jewish men. Or, the Beatle-like sideburns favored by many teen-agers. "The fellow in the PAIS is my younger son, Errol Flynn."

slivovitz (*slih* vuh vits) A potent plum wine served especially on holidays. Could be used to describe alcoholic beverages generally. "Miss Brewster, would you care to join me for a SLIVOVITZ?" "Joe is all right when he keeps away from the SLIVOVITZ."

trepverter (*trep* vair ter) A delightful term meaning all the clever things you think of to say five minutes after the opportunity has passed.

megilla (muh *gil* luh) A large scroll containing the Jewish law. Any reading matter or conversation that is long and tedious in its detail is a MEGILLA. Your maiden aunt's life story is a MEGILLA. Your child comes home late for supper, and instead of giving you a simple excuse, he tells you a MEGILLA.

You should have
a sweet death.
A barrel of sugar
should fall on your head.

6

Eat and Die

Among the world's cuisines, Jewish cooking is not exotic, not handsome, and certainly not fancy. However, it does have a unique quality. It's funny. It looks funny, and tastes funny (in the sense that it's fun to eat), and the Yiddish words for eating and food are funny words. But beware. Jewish food isn't funny at all when you've had too much of it.

bagel (*bay* gul) A doughnut-shaped bread roll. Tough as a snow tire. Surprisingly good taste. Never under any circumstances try to eat a stale one.

lox (locks) Smoked salmon. Looks mild. Tastes shockingly salty. Eat it late at night and nothing will help you. Not ice water, not Alka-Seltzer, not sleeping pills.

kishke (*kish* key) Stuffed derma (and *that's* the gut that covers sausage). If it tasted like it looks it would kill you instantly. Actually it has a pleasant, mild flavor, and the worst it can do you is heartburn.

knish (knish) Sweet chopped meat in a dough envelope. Eaten hot with the fingers or with a fork. For every three you eat, roughly one Alka-Seltzer.

matzo (*mot* suh) A large, unsalted cracker. Eaten plain, tastes slightly better than cardboard. In omlettes and dumplings very good, very filling.

gefilte fish (geh *fill* teh fish) Chopped whitefish, trout and carp rolled into irregular balls and served hot or cold, with horseradish. Another case of "if looks could kill." But delicious . . . and digestible!

blintz (blints) Cheese, potato or fruit wrapped in pancake dough and fried, then eaten with sour cream. Perhaps the world's most fattening food. Who has never tasted a BLINTZ has never gained five pounds in ten minutes.

kreplach (*krep* lach) The Jewish won ton. Meat in a small dough wrapper, served in chicken soup. Chicken KREPLACH soup is so rich and nourishing, it is said a man once drank three bowls and died from an excess of health.

shmaltz   (shmahlts)   Rendered chicken fat. This you'll have to make yourself. Smear it on some fresh bread. Sprinkle a little salt. Take a big bite and watch your arteries harden before your eyes.

halvah   (hol *vah*)   A confection of Near East origin, made of sesame. Sort of a sandy candy. Sticks in your teeth. Tastes good, even the next day.

farfel   (*fahr* fuhl)   Something half way between rice and noodles which is harmless enough in chicken soup, but all alone on a plate makes you wonder whether you should eat it or step on it.

kasha   (*kah* sha)   Cooked groats. An East European favorite that sinks to the bottom of chicken soup (what else?). Has the consistency of Grape Nuts.

chaleh   (*chah* leh)   Bread made with eggs and sprinkled with poppy seeds. If you're a bread lover, I can promise you no greater sensation than to push your nose deeply into the soft yellow heart of a warm, fresh-baked CHALEH.

flanken   (*flon* kin)   Very fat short ribs of beef, boiled to death, and served in a hunk. A popular dish (don't ask me why) found on every Jewish menu. To each his own, but I have always believed it tastes like wet socks.

holishkehs   (*hah* lish kehs)   Boiled cabbage stuffed with ground meat. An inexpensive and filling old-country dish that tastes like an inexpensive and filling old-country dish.

meichel for the beichel   (*my* chul . . . *by* chul)   A little gift for the tummy. After all, the stomach works hard, seldom complains, asks no favors. It should have a reward, too. Like a 2 A.M. snack maybe. Or a little extra dessert. A truly unselfish gesture and a hell of an excuse to overeat.

40

nosh (nahsh) To eat between meals. A useful word with no English equivalent. To eat between meals is not a good idea. To NOSH—though it means the same thing—is a grand idea. See the difference?

fress (fress) To eat with great gusto; to consume large amounts of food. Another convenient eating word. In English, a person who eats thus is called a pig. I, for one, would rather be called a FRESSER.

eppis essen (*ep* pis *es* sen) Something to eat. You take your parents out to Pierre's for coq au vin and truffles. They pick at their food. They would rather have EPPIS ESSEN.

brechvard (*brech* vard) Food so unappetizing as to make you sick. You are the dinner guest of a cosmopolitan friend, and you can't believe the soup. It's cream of goat soup, he says, a delicacy in Zanzibar. By you it's BRECHVARD.

trafe (*tray* feh) Forbidden (unclean) food. Even if you're not Jewish it's a good excuse, when somebody serves you cream of goat soup, to say, "Sorry, it's against my religion."

chazerai (chah zuh *rye*) Literally, pig's food. Junky, unsubstantial stuff. For lunch your daughter has caramel corn, marshmallows, pizza and red pop. Then she cries about pimples. Tell her, "You know why Dorian Gray had a face like that? Because he ate CHAZERAI!"

You should be killed by your mother-in-law right away.

7.

Funny, You Don't Look Gentile

Well, how are you doing? Can you say CHOCHEM without twisting your tonsils? Have you raised eyebrows at the office by calling the boss "a nice bloke but a SHTICK FETTS?" Good for you! You'll find that Yiddish is one up on other kinds of one-upmanship. And it beats beat-talk because it never goes out of fashion. Yiddish is the classic language of Hip.

But before you run out and overwhelm the first Gentile friend you see with Yiddish yammerings, here are a few more advanced idioms. If properly mastered, they will earn you a membership in that fast-growing organization known as GOYIM: Gentiles and Other Yiddish Insult Mavins.

veh is mir! (*vay* is mir) "I am pain itself!" A most melodramatic expression of suffering, used to describe everyday miseries such as shaving nicks, sinus headaches, or acid indigestion.

zol zein a zeh! (zol zine ah *zay*) "So let it be that way!" An expression of total resignation. "Goldwater is running again? ZOL ZEIN A ZEH!" "My wife had quintuplets? ZOL ZEÍN A ZEH!"

dos vakst a bum! (dahs vahkst ah *bum*) "There grows a bum!" What a father says of his son, whether it's because he made a girl pregnant or just because he left the front door open.

hock a chinick: (hock a *chy* nik*) To prattle; to go on incessantly about nothing. Your wife phones while you're in an important conference to tell you about a mouse in the dishwasher. "Don't HOCK ME A CHINICK," you say, and hang up.

---

* Exception. Pronounce the "ch" as in China.

oy gevalt! (oy geh *vahlt*) "May a great power intervene on my behalf!" Use in desperate situations like when you get a call from the Bureau of Internal Revenue or the kids uproot the neighbors' prize rose garden.

chob dir in bod! (chawb dir in *buhd*) A threat, meaning literally, "I'll get you in the bath!" A quaint notion certainly. And I'll leave it up to you to decide the next steps to take with your victim once you've got him in the tub.

vehr geharget! (*vehr* geh *har* get) "Drop dead!" A mild threat when you consider all the really colorful ways of killing somebody off in Yiddish.

ahlevai! (ah leh *vai*) "It should only be!" A seemingly hopeful exclamation which is actually an admission of hopelessness. The most gorgeous girl at the office party whispers in your ear, "You're too cute to be married." You whisper back, "AHLEVAI, baby!"

feh (feh) A word of disgust. Phooey! "Feh! They're dirty," says my mother of all animals. If she had her way, all house pets—dogs, pussycats, parakeets—would be made to fend for themselves in the jungle against lions, rhinoceri, and other germ-carrying beasts.

tokke (*tah* key) A common word of disbelief. Can it be? Would you believe? "If her daughter is so gorgeous, why did she marry a man without a nickel who is, TOKKE, seventy-five years old?"

genug shoen (guh *nook* shane) Enough already! Your daughter is making out the wedding invitation list. She's at 400 and only down to the "L's" when you tell her, "GENUG SHOEN. Even Westminster Abbey has fire regulations."

pahvolyeh   (pah *vole* yeh)   "Be careful!" "Look out!" You are suffering the discomforts of proctoscopy. You've already used up the normal vocabulary of pain, "Ooh! Ouch! Yeeha! Christ-amighty!" Try PAHVOLYEH! Maybe the doctor will have mercy and withdraw his COCKAMEHMEH instrument.

gornisht helfin!   (*gore* nisht *hell* fin)   "Nothing will help!" An expression of utter hopelessness. To illustrate how Yiddish keeps its sense of humor even in the depths of despair, the story is told of a man about to leap from the Brooklyn Bridge. A newspaper reporter asked him his name. "G. Helfin," he said, and jumped.

nu   (noo)   The most eloquent word in any language. Given a variety of inflections, it can mean almost anything you want it to. As a question: "Nu? So what?" As a challenge: "Nu! Show me!" As a triple-emphatic tongue-clucker: "NU NU NU! I told you so." And, if on your death bed, no memorable last words come to mind, just look up at your family, smile enigmatically, and say "Nu?" They'll spend the rest of their lives wondering what you meant.

Yiddish English

If you are charmed by the sound and meaning of Yiddish words but puzzled about how to work them into ordinary English conversation, let me assure you there is nothing easier. Yiddish is, perhaps, the ideal pidgin-language because it naturally assumes the syntax of the host language. In spicing your English vocabulary with Yiddish, the general rule is: don't think about grammar; use Yiddish words just as you would English words.

For instance: "Today, I SHLEP the kids to the Museum of Natural History. Yesterday, I SHLEPPED them to the zoo. Tomorrow, I'll be SHLEPPING around on crutches." Yiddish and English verbs are perfectly interchangeable.

Yiddish nouns are equally simple to use. Although you sometimes see them with the plural ending "im," as in GOYIM or MOMSERIM, in all cases the simple addition of the letter "s" or "es" produces acceptable Yiddish plurals for use with English. Goys and MOMSERS are fine. PUTZES and KLUTZES are dandy. Most verbs can be changed handily to nouns by the addition of the suffix "er." Hence, SHLEP becomes SHLEPER. KIBBITZ becomes KIBBITZER, and SHPRITZ becomes SHPRITZER.

As for adjectives, simply use them as you find them in this book.

In order to make it easier for you to commit Yiddish words to memory, in some cases I have ignored the most common English spelling. For example, all entries in this book having the initial letters "sh" are generally listed in English dictionaries under "sch":

> shnorer——schnorrer
> shtick——schtick
> shlep——schlepp

Yiddish prefixes and suffixes are also spelled and pronounced variously. For instance, VERBLONGET can be FARBLONGET; GEHSHTRUFT is sometimes VERSHTRUFT or even FARSHTRUFT; and FERIMMTER may be BERIMMTER. Words like NAHFKEH and BUMMERKEH may be pronounced NAHFKEY and BUMMERKEY. Take your pick.

Although I doubt whether such refined information is of use to you, I include it in the event you find yourself speaking Litvak in the presence of a Galitzianer (in which case you will encounter numerous other variations) or vice versa. Also, many a popular Jewish novelist indulges in a Yiddishism now and then, and their spellings are likely to be as inconsistent as my own.

46

Index of Words

Picture credits: Culver (pages 10, 32, 42);